For King and Crown

Conversations on the Christian Life

Other books by Michael Duncan

Starting Out: A Study Guide for New Believers

A Life Worth Living (Booklet)

Shadows: Book of Aleth, Part One

Revelation: Book of Aleth, Part Two

Shadow Remnant

From Vision to Victory

A Golfer's Guide to Christianity

~~~

For more books from Michael Duncan, or to contact him visit his website at:

www.authormichaelduncan.com.
~~~

For King and Crown

Conversations on the Christian Life

Michael Duncan

For King and Crown
Conversations on the Christian Life

ISBN-13: 979-8533090803

Table of Contents

PROLOGUE

FOR KING AND CROWN

As you open the pages of this little book, I want to address a couple of questions that you may have. They were asked of me as I wrote it and they may occur to you as well.

First, is this an autobiography?

No, this is not an autobiography, though there are several places where I express some of my own experiences and offer some insights into my own thoughts. I'm not really convinced that my story is of any consequence except that it shows the work and love of Christ in my life.

I find that people who write their stories often do so with the intent to express a view of their own importance or significance in this world. After I'm gone, if someone wants to write my biography, they can do as they wish. And I may even share some more details of my life in future writings. However, my intention would still be to use my life experiences as the springboard to point you to Jesus.

Second, is this a counseling book?

Well, to answer that would depend on what type of counseling you mean. I'm not a counselor or a therapist. I am a pastor, husband, father, etc., and I love the Lord word so that you can discover Christ in greater measure. And, if you will permit me, I'd like to borrow a prayer from the Apostle Paul that is my prayer also for you.

> *And so, from the day we heard, we have not ceased to pray for you, asking that you may be filled with the knowledge of his will in all spiritual wisdom and understanding, so as to walk in a manner worthy of the Lord, fully pleasing to him: bearing fruit in every good work and increasing in the knowledge of God; being strengthened with all power, according to his glorious might, for all endurance and patience with joy; giving thanks to the Father, who has qualified you to share in the inheritance of the saints in light. He has delivered us from the domain of darkness and transferred us to the*

kingdom of his beloved Son, in whom we have redemption, the forgiveness of sins. ~ Colossians 1:9-14

Your Servant in Christ,

Michael

My life is set for King and crown

The King on high of great renown

The crown of life He promised me

For King and crown my life shall be.

~ M. Duncan

Chapter One

Who Am I?

I am a wretched sinner.

It's not hard to say that, for the truth is actually quite easy when you get used to it. I could paint a picture of my life that would destroy any potential pedestal standing.

Most people can.

But it is not in our nature to want to expose the real, broken reality that we are. From my observation, most people today never want to admit it. People spend a lot of effort to try and convince themselves and others that their lives are pristine, unstained with the reality of sin. And when that doesn't work, they will point to others that are more necrotic then themselves.

When our ability to convince ourselves that we are genuinely good begins to fail, we surround ourselves with people and voices that will trumpet a cacophony of praise. We tune in to those pastors who preach our worthiness. We seek out counselors to console us with self-importance. We listen to therapists who incessantly teach that without us the world might just come to an end.

In fact, humanity seems to be abuzz with glowing words of self-affirmation. But what is the truth? Who am I, really?

Have you ever asked that question?

There is an old, philosophical statement that asks: "Is this all that I am, is there nothing more?" I remember many years ago, while I was still in grade school, hearing that question posited in an English class. I've been asking that question ever since.

The one answer I keep pounding my head against is the simple statement of the Apostle Paul in 1 Timothy 1:15, "*The saying is trustworthy and deserving of full acceptance, that Christ Jesus came into the world to save sinners, of whom I am the foremost.*"

Again, in a similar expression of truth, Paul said, "*Wretched man that I am*" (Romans 7:24).

Long before I was a Christian, before those declarations from God's word ever reached my mind and heart, I knew by instinct it was true of me. For all my effort to try and believe better about myself, I knew different: I was wretched... a sinner. I didn't know why!

Well, perhaps, in some respects I did know why.

As a young boy, I walked with my sister to a small church meeting in a home down the street from us. Later, I attended some Catholic masses with my family. As a teen I participated in a weekly Christian youth event. And without knowing it, the Biblical truth of my sinful condition was planted in my heart like a seed.

Though I hadn't at that point made any effort to read the Bible in a serious way, the grip of that truth hounded me throughout my adolescence and dogged my steps into young adulthood. And with that subconscious identifier neatly tucked away in my mind, I stumbled along the road of my life, tripping through the potholes of depression and despair.

But, isn't self-deprecation just as tragic as self-adulation? A haughty disposition is dreadful, and arrogance is ugly. But isn't self-scorn another debilitating construct of our human experience? These questions also ruminated in my thoughts as I continued the contemplation of self.

For in this world I have seen those who perceive themselves with such a morose attitude that they cannot even consider the idea that they have value. And, in truth, I've been down that road as well.

Depression and self-hate marked some of the steps in my journey through life. I've found such conditions to be far more damaging in the immediate moment, causing many people to inflict physical harm on themselves. Pride does go before destruction, but that destruction doesn't always manifest in the immediate moment. Melancholy can also bring destruction, and sometimes that damage is done right away.

So, what do we do? What is the curative process for unmitigated despair? Yep... you're right, we head right back to the therapists and counselors who will try with all their skill to boost our egos with a barrage of praise. We turn to consultants who give us a multitude of processes to think better of ourselves.

And the dance continues: self-love, self-hate, the "psychoanalysis two-step." All the while, the question is yet to be answered: who am I?

Without an answer to that unrelenting question, I began to look around at the people who pass through my life and wonder if I need to simply become like them? Should I follow the crowd? Or, perhaps, maybe find someone who I think is better than me and do what they do?

Maybe I'll assuage my conscience with this notion: at least I'm not as bad as "them," whoever the "them" is. However, I'm told never to compare myself to others because, “comparison is the key to self-defeat.” Well, that is an interesting quote since all my life I’ve seen the entire world strive in comparison to each other.

Speaking of comparisons, have you ever noticed that one of the major attempts in advertising campaigns is to parade a bevy of perfect-looking human specimens across the television or on social media platforms in order to show you what could happen if you just used their product or bought their program? “This is what YOU could be like if you only...” and the ad continues.

Marketing ploys are set to display the successful in front of the up-and-comers that they should “gaze upon their potential future.”

This even happens in the fellowship of Christians.

Churches gather in conventions to compare notes and make assessments as to who is the best of the bunch based upon their numbers. Pastors sit in council with each other for the sole purpose of making sure they are able to bask in the lime-light. The virtue of faithfulness is extoled, provided that such faithfulness is marked by measurable success. And yet as I look upon all these things I have been a party to, I am ashamed of the fact that this is what we are reduced to.

Pride, shame, arrogance, jealousy.

I've known all these things in my life, and have been hurt by each. And yet I continue to pound my proverbial fist against the ever persistent question: "who am I?!"

The world doesn't offer an answer. My friends cannot provide any illumination. Counselors and advertisers alike all try to mask the reality under the shell of self-improvement.

I turned to the Scriptures to find the answer. It is the only source of truth that will deal with me honestly, clearly and without reservation. And in that most holy book I have learned a dreadful truth – I am not just a wretched man, I am a prisoner in my wretchedness.

Consider the grand dilemma of the Apostle Paul:

> *So I find it to be a law that when I want to do right, evil lies close at hand. For I delight in the law of God, in my inner being, but I see in my members another law waging war against the law of my mind and making me captive to the law of sin that dwells in my members. Wretched man that I am! Who will deliver me from this body of death? ~ Romans 7:21-24*

It gets worse.

I'm not in a holding cell awaiting trial; I'm not on remand until my court date with heaven. I have already been found guilty. I am a condemned criminal, sentenced to death by the court of Almighty God.

But wait! I don't "feel" guilty. I look at all the abusers of life around me and I think to myself that I cannot possibly be facing the same sentence they will suffer. Then the words of the Apostle Paul race in my mind.

> *For I am not aware of anything against myself, but I am not thereby acquitted. It is the Lord who judges me. ~ 1 Corinthians 4:4*

My conscience is of no use if I try to declare my innocence before God! He is the judge and according to the Word of God, that judgment has already been passed down to all the inhabitants of the earth:

> *"Whoever believes in him is not condemned, but whoever does not believe is condemned already, because he has not believed in the name of the only Son of God."*
> *~ John 3:18*

But wait! Hold on just a second! There is hope in that declaration of our Lord. He said condemnation is for those who *don't* believe.

I DO BELIEVE!

I believe in the Son of God, the Lord Jesus Christ. I believe that He alone is the hope of salvation and that through His shed blood on the cross He paid for my sins. I believe He endured the wrath of God for me, and bore the full measure of all the judgment I deserved. He promised all who look to the Son will have life—and I believe it!

And suddenly I'm released!

I am no longer under the sentence of death. I have been freed from my condemnation, acquitted by the Judge Himself for there was One who stood in my place and received all God's wrath that was meant for me. Jesus Christ, the Righteous One was condemned as a sinner so that He could take the place of any who will believe on Him.

Now, however, my heart is crushed under the weight of self-condemnation as I look upon the Holy One of God who bore the cross, the shame, the sentence of death, and the wrath of God. I am unworthy! I don't deserve such love. Why would He do all that for me?

Oh such love, such grace. Beyond any measure I could possibly comprehend, the Lord Jesus Christ showed His love for me when I, a wretched sinner and bound for hell. I was received by Him and made to be His. He cut the chains that bound me to death and liberated me from the just punishment that awaited me. His mercy made me new, His grace saved me. To the depths of my soul I will forever be amazed and filled with praise for His love toward me.

The whole world of "Atta-boy" counselors could never come close to helping me discover the joy I found in that moment when I looked to the Savior and He rescued me. The entire chorus of humanity could sing my praise and it would never measure up to the heart-flood of joy I will receive when the King of kings tells me, "well done." And when my own heart begins to sink into the darkened abyss of self-condemnation, I simply have to recall His word that says:

> *By this we shall know that we are of the truth and reassure our heart before him; for whenever our heart condemns us, God is greater than our heart, and he knows everything. ~ 1 John 3:19-20*

Who am I? I am a child of God.

Chapter Two

Who is God?

Let's be honest, we are terrified of really knowing God.

Why would I say that? All around us are the testimonies of those who declare that God is this loving, generous, caring, sustaining, benevolent and merciful Deity that does nothing more than lavish upon the world His abounding provision. We see His glory in sunsets and experience His sweetness in the gentle spring rains.

Everything stated above is true. Absolutely true. God is profusely kind and richly merciful. He loves beyond measure and He sustains all things. He abounds His grace toward us in lavish abundance.

So why would I say that we are actually terrified to really know God?

Because knowing God is life-shattering.

Most people have a comfortable conception of who God is, despite the fact that He has revealed Himself in the pages of the Holy Bible. Consider all the false gods that have been invented throughout the history of mankind. What is the predominant reality of any false God? They are silent in their expressions, impotent in their power, and useless as a god. Even so, people flock to their version or form of a false deity and believe it will offer them the option of self-improvement, even autonomy. What else would you expect from a man-made god?

In fact, it's easy to obey a self-invented god. Any personal imagination of a divine being will always allow you to conform to the myriad desires of the human heart. Why? Simple: you invented it so you get to make the rules.

But the true God, the Almighty and Creator of all things, the One who sustains life and provides salvation is beyond our limited comprehension and outside of our feeble control. And knowing Him will radically alter every miniscule detail of our lives.

I think most would prefer God to be a little less almighty and more controllable. But the true God is *the* authority. He will not obey the will of man nor conform to the desires of our sinful nature.

Consider the words of the Psalmist:

> *"These things you have done, and I have been silent; you thought that I was one like yourself. But now I rebuke you and lay the charge before you. Mark this, then, you who forget God, lest I tear you apart, and there be none to deliver! The one who offers thanksgiving as his sacrifice glorifies me; to one who orders his way rightly I will show the salvation of God!"* ~ *Psalm 50:21-23*

I highly recommend you read the entirety of the Psalm stated above. God is nothing like us. And it is the reality of God's absolute justice and righteousness that sets the human heart to tremble. We'd much prefer God to be managed by our whims and imaginations.

But we must look to God revealed in Scripture, and not the god of human fancies. The Almighty wants a relationship with mankind and He is the one who made it possible. The only way such a relationship can occur is when humanity finally casts off their false ponderings and bow humbly before Him.

Read it for yourself from the prophet Isaiah:

> *For thus says the One who is high and lifted up, who inhabits eternity, whose name is Holy: "I dwell in the high and holy place, and also with him who is of a contrite and lowly spirit, to revive the spirit of the lowly, and to revive the heart of the contrite."* ~ *Isaiah 57:15*

Go back to the opening of this chapter and let's be honest. Everything stated there sounds more like a Hallmark™ card than an actual relationship? We've all sent those cards to our family and friends, those sentimental expressions of personal connections. And when people send them to us we think, “oh, how nice.”

Hmmm... Is that how we view God? Do we come to into Divine fellowship with more sentimentality than actual engagement?

I’ve given greeting cards to my wife, but is that the summation of our relationship with each other? Isn’t there something between a husband and wife deeper and more profound? And if that’s the case concerning our closest human relationship, there must be more to truly knowing God than mere sentimentality.

But deep in our hearts we don’t want to actually know God, because to know Him who is the Creator of the universe, Sustainer of all things, and Savior of our souls is, in truth, terrifying.

Why? Because it will radically change us forever.

We can't even exist in the same dimension as God. Our sinful, selfish, broken, vile and wretched selves cannot possibly stand before the Holiness on high. He is TERRIFYING! And if we are to encounter Him in the majestic truth of His being, we can never walk away from that encounter without being drastically altered.

So we set God aside and pick up our Hallmark version of Him and go merrily on our way without any qualms about who He is because we have made the God of Creation manageable.

Do you know what the problem is? Of course you do. Our manageable version of the Almighty isn't real. We've invented a god of our own design and worship something that isn't true.

This is reflective of what Isaiah warned against in the creating of our own version of God.

> *They know not, nor do they discern, for he has shut their eyes, so that they cannot see, and their hearts, so that they cannot understand. No one considers, nor is there knowledge or discernment to say, "Half of it I burned in the fire; I also baked bread on its coals; I roasted meat and have eaten. And shall I make the rest of it an abomination? Shall I fall down before a block of wood?" ~ Isaiah 44:18-19*

There is no hope found in a false god. There is no salvation ever offered by the imaginations of our own mind. No one has ever become pleasing to the Lord by creating an idol.

We need to encounter God.

We are desperate without Him and if we ignore the truth of God we will forever be trapped in the deception of our sin. We must run the risk of encounter, or be lost forever.

But God is not the one hiding. We are.

Consider the Scriptures below concerning man's effort to hide from God.

- *(Adam) And he said, "I heard the sound of you in the garden, and I was afraid, because I was naked, and I hid myself." ~ Genesis 3:10*
- *(Moses) And he said, "I am the God of your father, the God of Abraham, the God of Isaac, and the God of Jacob." And Moses hid his face, for he was afraid to look at God. ~ Exodus 3:6*
- *(Peter) But when Simon Peter saw it, he fell down at Jesus' knees, saying, "Depart from me, for I am a sinful man, O Lord." ~ Luke 5:8*

Either we will try to hide or we will want God to go away because in His illuminating presence there is an absolute certainty our sins will be exposed. So, if you think you had an encounter with God and you are not radically altered, can you be certain it *was* an encounter with God?

But who is this God?

I'm going to take you to three places in the Bible. On each of these mountains God reveals Himself and it is my prayer that from these encounters you grow in your comprehension of God.

Place number one: Mount Sinai.

> *On the morning of the third day there were thunders and lightnings and a thick cloud on the mountain and a very loud trumpet blast, so that all the people in the camp trembled. Then Moses brought the people*

> *out of the camp to meet God, and they took their stand at the foot of the mountain. Now Mount Sinai was wrapped in smoke because the Lord had descended on it in fire. The smoke of it went up like the smoke of a kiln, and the whole mountain trembled greatly. And as the sound of the trumpet grew louder and louder, Moses spoke, and God answered him in thunder. The Lord came down on Mount Sinai, to the top of the mountain. And the Lord called Moses to the top of the mountain, and Moses went up. – Exodus 19:16-20*

Place number two: The Mount of Transfiguration.

> *And after six days Jesus took with him Peter and James, and John his brother, and led them up*

a high mountain by themselves. And he was transfigured before them, and his face shone like the sun, and his clothes became white as light. And behold, there appeared to them Moses and Elijah, talking with him. And Peter said to Jesus, "Lord, it is good that we are here. If you wish, I will make three tents here, one for you and one for Moses and one for Elijah." He was still speaking when, behold, a bright cloud overshadowed them, and a voice from the cloud said, "This is my beloved Son, with whom I am well pleased; listen to him." When the disciples heard this, they fell on their faces and were terrified.
~ Matthew 17:1-6

Place number three: The Mount of Glory

And he carried me away in the Spirit to a great, high mountain, and showed me the holy city Jerusalem coming down out of heaven from God... And I saw no temple in the city, for its temple is the Lord God the Almighty and the Lamb. And the city has no need of sun or moon to shine on it, for the glory of God gives it light, and its lamp is the Lamb. By its light will the nations walk, and the kings of the earth will bring their glory into it, and its gates will never be shut by day—and there will be no night there. They will bring into it the glory and the honor of the nations. But nothing unclean will ever enter it, nor anyone who does what is detestable or false, but only those who are written in the Lamb's

> *book of life. ~ Revelation 21:10, 22-27*

Stand on these mountains for just a moment and tremble in the radiance of God Almighty.

If you do not know God, my friends, He is far more than the sentimental deity that is often delivered to you. He is Almighty. He is Creator. He is King of kings and Lord of lords. He is holy, righteous and completely perfect.

And, perhaps the most terrifying... He Is JUDGE.

> *He who sits in the heavens laughs; the Lord holds them in derision. Then he will speak to them in his wrath, and terrify them in his fury, saying, "As for me, I have set my King on Zion, my holy hill." ~ Psalm 2:4-6*

Take a moment right now and go to Psalm 2. Read the entire thing. Hear God speak to you that you should come to His Son, the Lord Jesus, and yield yourself to Him.

> *Kiss the Son lest he be angry, and you perish in the way, for his wrath is quickly kindled. Blessed are all who take refuge in him. ~ Psalm 2:12*

Be fearful of God, and draw near to Him anyway. Know that you will be radically altered in your life. Your knowledge, your insights, your wisdom and your very sense of self will all dramatically change when you truly encounter God.

There is no possibility for me to try and convey to you in this little chapter the magnificence and majesty of Almighty God. Go to the place He has revealed Himself, the Holy Bible, and start hiking up those mountains with Moses, the prophets, the disciples and all who desired to know the Living God.

Who is God? I'll let Him speak it for Himself:

> *God said to Moses, "I am who I am." And he said, "Say this to the people of Israel: 'I am has sent me to you.'"* ~ *Exodus 3:14*

> *Jesus said to them, "Truly, truly, I say to you, before Abraham was, I am."* ~ *John 8:58*

Chapter Three
Why the Bible?

I love the Bible.

By now you've already read many times that I reference the Bible for the answers I need.

Over and over again I am drawn to that holy book for insight into the human condition, the needs of my own heart and the direction necessary to continue in life.

That collection of sixty-six books which cover the gamut of human history – from the creation of mankind to the final redemption of Christ – is my foundation and my filter for all aspects of life. In fact, everyone in all of this human experience builds their life upon some foundation and filters their experiences through some form of wisdom.

Why the Bible? Other "holy" books are out there. The Koran, the Bhagavad Gita and others religious tomes fill up the shelves of humanity. Aren't they just as good at giving guidance to the human experience?

Simply put: no.

What about science? Doesn't scientific study and a systematic methodology of logical apprehension provide a reasonable resource? In truth, there are those who adhere to "science" more like a religion. I put that in quotes because true science ought to be a serious and rigorous exploration for the truth and not a religious pursuit. However, in the current climate of societal development many of the modern scientists are more akin to function as "priests of humanism" rather than arduous explorers in search of truth. This fracturing of scientific methodology is leading mankind down a path of pseudo religious observance rather than intellectual discovery.

The notion of "following the science" has become the mantra and cadence call of many, provided that the "science" is in accord and agreement with the current philosophical mentality. Otherwise, it is silenced in the cancel-culture of the modern era.

In the culture of inclusivism, isn't it better to just compile a collection of religious doctrines and humanistic practices? Basically, build something that agrees with the whims and will of self or something that satisfies the mainstream mentality. If you've driven anywhere you have probably seen bumper stickers that display a variety of religious symbols of the world. They are organized in such a way that it creates a word which some might believe is the best option.

That word is: "Coexist."

And why not? Can't we blend the various substantive ideas from the world's religions and create some kind of amalgam that satisfies the human desire for a religious life?

I am reminded of a time when my mom would make an oil and vinegar dressing. She would combine the ingredients in a bottle and then shake it vigorously, even violently, to force the elements into a mixture that you could pour on your salad. However, let the bottle rest a moment and the components in the container would separate and finally settle into their respective places. They never actually became a unique singular liquid. They were mixed, shaken, and coaxed into a concoction that would always and ultimately divide.

And that is the way of blending doctrines from a variety of religious ideologies. The will never coalesce, but must separate into their unique dispositions.

But why is the Bible of such dramatic importance to me? And not just to me, I am convinced that it is absolutely necessary for the entire world.

Why do I love the Bible? Let me explain.

First, I love the Bible because it tells the truth.

The argument is made by many that other religious texts tell "truths" that can be used to make their lives better. But the Bible tells THE TRUTH.

The psalmist makes this abundantly clear.

> *The law of the Lord is perfect, reviving the soul; the testimony of the Lord is sure, making wise the simple; the precepts of the Lord are right, rejoicing the heart; the commandment of the Lord is pure, enlightening the eyes; the fear of the Lord is clean, enduring forever; the rules of the Lord are true, and righteous altogether. More to be desired are they than gold, even much fine gold; sweeter also than honey and drippings of the honeycomb. Moreover, by them is your servant warned; in keeping them there is great reward. ~ Psalm 19:7-11*

It doesn't just provide religious guidance on how to have a better life. The Bible, the

Word of God, speaks the truth and it reveals the core condition of man without reservation or hesitation.

It doesn't try to make me feel better so that I will like it; the Bible exposes me to the very darkness of my soul. Consider the indictment found in the book of Romans that is leveled at the whole human race:

> *As it is written: None is righteous, no, not one; no one understands; no one seeks for God. All have turned aside; together they have become worthless; no one does good, not even one. Their throat is an open grave; they use their tongues to deceive. The venom of asps is under their lips. Their mouth is full of curses and bitterness. Their feet are swift to shed blood; in their paths are ruin and misery, and the way of peace they have not known. There is no*

fear of God before their eyes. ~ Romans 3:10-16

So you might be asking at this point: why would I love the Word of God when it tells me I'm bad? Because, as stated in chapter one, I know I'm bad – wretched as a matter of fact – and now I can understand why. The Bible is very clear on this point.

But more than just exposing the reality of my wickedness, I love the Word of God because it also illuminates what Christ did in order to deliver me from my sin. And it doesn't hinge on me become more "religious."

Religion is useless to save a soul. And the world is filled with religion. And my soul needed saving. The Bible brings to light the way of salvation, through faith in the Lord Jesus and His atoning work. He suffered the wrath of God for the sin of man, and all who will believe and trust Jesus, yielding their life to Him, can be saved.

For all have sinned and fall short of the glory of God, and are justified by his grace as a gift, through the redemption that is in Christ Jesus, whom God put forward as a propitiation by his blood, to be received by faith. This was to show God's righteousness, because in his divine forbearance he had passed over former sins. ~ Romans 3:23-25

Second, I love the Bible because it reveals God.

Atheists do not believe God exists. “Secular” scientists say that God cannot be discovered. And false religions invent a variety of gods that are more reflective of man than anything else.

But I look around and notice that creation is filled with creativity and controlled with a sense of order. Planets don’t go careening into suns, life blooms according to their coded internal programing called DNA. Complex design is strewn throughout the world around me—and in me. The vast expanse of the universe cannot be measured with any accuracy, and the depths of life cannot be fathomed.

Everywhere I look there is order, design, complexity and imagination. Now I have caused some accidents in my day (not all have been my fault). One thing is true, no matter how many times an accident occurs, it does not end in a greater sense of order and beauty!

The absolute grandeur of this universe demands the observer to understand: this is no accident.

Seeing the vastness of creation I have to believe that there is a God who is greater still. An eternal God, an omniscient God, an all-powerful God who created this whole thing. A creator is never less than their creation, so the One who created all things must be beyond comprehension.

The Bible says just that – God is beyond our ability to grasp. He must reveal Himself and if He doesn't then there is no possibility that we, who cannot even grasp the vastness of the universe or the complexity of life, will ever be able to comprehend God.

And, guess what? God reveals Himself in the Scriptures – and in no greater way than in the incarnation of Jesus Christ.

> *Long ago, at many times and in many ways, God spoke to our fathers by the prophets, but in these last days he has spoken to us by his Son, whom he appointed the heir of all things, through whom also he created the world. He is the radiance of the glory of God and the exact imprint of his nature, and he upholds the*

> *universe by the word of his power. ~ Hebrews 1:1-3a*

And now, third, I love the Bible because it reveals the Savior and Lord – Jesus Christ.

All the promises of the Old Testament point our view toward the fulfillment of those promises in the New Testament, and those promises are fulfilled in Christ. Paul said as much to the church in Corinth.

> *For all the promises of God find their Yes in him. That is why it is through him that we utter our Amen to God for his glory. ~ 2 Corinthians 1:20*

Jesus, Himself, said as much.

> *"You search the Scriptures because you think that in them you have eternal life; and it is they that bear witness about me." ~ John 5:39*

Understand that there is no other way to be saved except through Jesus Christ. You may ask why? Because: there is no way for me or you to atone for our rebellion against God. We need to be saved from the wrath of God, for God's wrath is kindled against sin and it will burn the world in His fiery judgment that will eventually come to this world.

Jesus took upon Himself the entirety of God's wrath – bearing it on the cross that He should be the full payment for sin for all who will believe.

Consider what Paul says in Romans:

> *"...but God shows his love for us in that while we were still sinners, Christ died for us. Since, therefore, we have now been justified by his blood, much more shall we be saved by him from the wrath of God. For if while we were enemies we were reconciled to God by the death of his Son,*

> *much more, now that we are reconciled, shall we be saved by his life."* ~ *Romans 5:8-10*

And, now, being born-again and found in Christ, the fourth reason I love the Bible: it gives clear direction for my life.

Admittedly, I do not fulfill the will of God in any way that is perfect. I am still a sinner, saved by grace and delivered from His wrath. Still I find when I try to make my own way I am always headed in the wrong direction. When I turn to God's word and follow the Scriptures in obedience to the Lord Jesus, I am always on the right path – even if I stumble along that path. God, through the prophet Jeremiah gave us this promise:

> *Thus says the Lord: "Stand by the roads, and look, and ask for the ancient paths, where the good way is; and walk in it, and find*

> *rest for your souls." ~ Jeremiah 6:16a*

Jesus is the fulfillment of that promise.

> *"Take my yoke upon you, and learn from me, for I am gentle and lowly in heart, and you will find rest for your souls." ~ Matthew 11:29*

It is on the "ancient paths" of obedience to God, learning from Jesus and following Him in faithfulness where that "rest" will be provided. It is the only direction that is worth going.

Ultimately, the Bible is the one book that provides all the wisdom necessary to know the way of salvation and the path of righteousness. It reveals God in His majesty. It exposes mankind to their sin. It calls all men to be saved and I heard that call. It points all mankind to Christ. And when I looked, I saw the glorious Savior. Forever I will exalt God's word.

Why do I love the Bible? For the reasons given, and many more.

Chapter Four

To Church or Not to Church

I have, in some regard, been a part of a church almost all my life. Early on I was brought to the Catholic church, going through the various stages of what young men deal with in confirmations and dedications, communions and confessions. I lit the candles, listened to the liturgies and in most respects basically fell asleep while the message was given.

This continued, on and off, until I was, perhaps, 12.

At the age of 19 I became a believer in Christ and began to attend church again. Unlike during my childhood, with a new-found faith in the Savior, I craved church fellowship. I participated in bible studies, attended multiple worship services during the week, joined the choir (I still should apologize to the various choir directors), and I grew.

Boy did I grow!

I fell in love with God's word, with the music of the Christian faith, with the harmonies of choral groups, with the multitude of fellowship gatherings (and pot-lucks!) and with sermons. I loved sermons. I still love sermons. In fact, I was listening to another one just moments ago. I could soak for hours in the faithful preaching of God's word.

One year, while still serving in the U.S. Air Force, I was sent overseas. Several Christian friends told me that when I returned, I would be shocked and, perhaps, disappointed with what I observed in the American church. They said my time in another country would radically alter my view of church.

And it did.

The Christians I encountered and the churches I experienced, in a land where Christianity hadn't become the popular and marketable franchises of the American culture, were filled with such vitality and a love for Jesus that I was humbled by their dedication to the Lord. Through these churches and their generous expressions of faith we built an orphanage, started multiple bible studies, did street witnessing, expressed worship and prayed. Oh how we prayed! There was no fund raising. No one recruited anyone to "lend a hand." No cajoling for volunteers to go downtown with the gospel. Needs were expressed and people were moved to accomplish God's love.

Consider what the Scripture says.

> *And let us not grow weary of doing good, for in due season we will reap, if we do not give up. So then, as we have opportunity, let us do good to everyone, and especially to those who are of the household of faith. ~ Galatians 6:9-10*

In that foreign country, I witnessed the above text come to light in the life of the church. To give you an example, at the site for the orphanage, I showed up, along with a bevy of volunteers, and we waited on an empty concrete slab. I asked the interpreter how long we should wait before giving up, for it seemed that no one was coming. He told me to wait, and watch.

Twenty minutes later a truck rolled up with lumber. Then another truck drove up with plumbing parts then another with roofing materials. One by one, those who were Christians and owned lumber yards or electrical wiring companies, painters and plumbers, and suddenly I was surrounded by the church! Each man or woman gave what they were able and offered their skills. To my surprise, in less than ten hours an orphanage was assembled. Nobody coordinated it. It was mentioned in church and told where to go.

And they just came. It seemed to me they understood the reality of what James had stated:

So whoever knows the right thing to do and fails to do it, for him it is sin. ~ James 4:17

They knew the right thing to do... and they did it.

When I returned to the States and entered into the fellowship of a church near the base where I was stationed, the disenchantment became almost unbearable.

Rather than worship, prayer and the preaching of the word, much of the fellowship focused on the latest and greatest experience that fed their emotions.

Fund raisers resounded from the pulpit for this project or that project.

Pleadings rang out for volunteers to care for the young in the nursery.

Phone calls issued from the pastor to high-profile performers, inviting them to perform in order that they might bring larger crowds into the church building.

My heart sank.

I longed to return to the simplicity of service and sacrifice I experienced overseas. And there, while seated in the crowd at church, my conscience was hit by an overwhelming drive to do something in my own land.

I saw something in the American church that Paul warned the Corinthians against.

> *But I am afraid that as the serpent deceived Eve by his cunning, your thoughts will be led astray from a sincere and pure devotion to Christ. ~ 2 Corinthians 11:3*

That "sincere and pure devotion" seemed lost in the fog of worldly efforts to accomplish spiritual tasks.

Now, please don't think that I see this in EVERY church gathering in America. Truly it's not. Though the marketing mentality of the culture and the commercialized condition of the American mindset seeps into the churches quite often, yet many church fellowships haven't fallen prey to such dilemmas.

What was I going to do? You're right.

I turned to the word of God. I needed to know the church from God's point of view. I needed to see it from His word.

The first place I encounter even the use of the word "church" is in Matthew 16.

> *He said to them, "But who do you say that I am?" Simon Peter replied, "You are the Christ, the Son of the living God." And Jesus answered him, "Blessed are you, Simon Bar-Jonah! For flesh and blood has not revealed this to*

> *you, but my Father who is in heaven. And I tell you, you are Peter, and on this rock I will build my church, and the gates of hell shall not prevail against it." ~ Matthew 16:15-18*

What a promise! Christ, Himself, will build the church and even the gates of hell will not be able to stand in opposition. Immediately I abandoned all the marketing ploys and manipulations of worldly endeavors and purposed to embrace the rock solid foundation of God's word as the source for the church.

Now, as I write this, I am ruminating on thirty years of public ministry behind me (and many more in front of me by God's grace). I must confess that I have fallen prey to the drive to see more people in attendance, the jealousy of other "successes" when I've struggled along, and the dalliance into some salesmanship models that I once again heartily reject as unprofitable in God's kingdom.

I am encouraged and challenged by Paul's charge to Timothy.

> *I charge you in the presence of God and of Christ Jesus, who is to judge the living and the dead, and by his appearing and his kingdom: preach the word; be ready in season and out of season; reprove, rebuke, and exhort, with complete patience and teaching. For the time is coming when people will not endure sound teaching, but having itching ears they will accumulate for themselves teachers to suit their own passions. ~ 2 Timothy 4:1-3*

As I look back on those early and formative years, I am reminded of that time when I fell in love with God's word and the preaching of it. Those many, many... MANY years ago in that church where I grew in Christ. That's what I wanted, that's what I longed for and loved. And that, my friends, is what I strive to be—faithful to Christ and His word.

If we are going to discover anything about the church, let us gaze upon the first church – found in the book of Acts.

> *And with many other words he bore witness and continued to exhort them, saying, "Save yourselves from this crooked generation." So those who received his word were baptized, and there were added that day about three thousand souls.*
>
> *And they devoted themselves to the apostles' teaching and the fellowship, to the breaking of bread and the prayers. And awe came upon every soul, and many wonders and signs were being*

done through the apostles. And all who believed were together and had all things in common. And they were selling their possessions and belongings and distributing the proceeds to all, as any had need. And day by day, attending the temple together and breaking bread in their homes, they received their food with glad and generous hearts, praising God and having favor with all the people. And the Lord added to their number day by day those who were being saved. ~ Acts 2:40-47

As you've just read about that first church gathered in Jerusalem and the thousands that were saved that day, how does the modern church compare? Even now I'm thinking of my own fellowship and examining my own heart to make sure that same devotion of the early church is paramount in ours.

I've had many people tell me that they "don't need to go to church to be a Christian." I can't possibly get to the depths of how wrong that statement is. But I will put it very plainly. You don't "go to church." You gather with the church, you ARE the church. The Sunday collective worship, of gathering to offer our praise and prayers, to hearken to the preaching of God's word, will never be experienced by someone with a "go to church" mentality. The concept of the "go to church" idea is not found in the Scriptures, but is built upon the theater-driven, entertainment hunger of a world oversaturated with commercials.

The first church gathering, oh they were devoted! They loved the Lord. They loved each other and found great strength in the fellowship of the saints of Christ. They hungered for God's word, proclaimed by the apostles, and sought opportunities to minister to and sacrifice for the needs of others. They had left the world for the Lord and discovered, to their joy, those who were with them stood closer than family.

And maybe that's why people don't like to "go to church." In the modern American church, rigged with light shows and pithy pseudo-psychology, nobody ever experiences what they did in that first church – the majesty of Jesus and the magnificence of a people who truly are devoted to all things concerning Him.

I look back and realize that I sit upon a mountain of precious examples: My first pastor, a powerful man of God who preaches the word without hesitation; My overseas experiences, helping me to see the radical nature of real church; My return to the States that opened my eyes to the tragedy of a commercialized church; And my many years of struggles and strivings, of disasters and delights that even now remind me to let the word of God remain the central core of all that is the church.

Let me remind you of how God's word describes the church.

> *I hope to come to you soon, but I am writing these things to you so that, if I delay, you may know how one ought to behave in the household of God, which is the church of the living God, a pillar and buttress of the truth. ~ 1 Timothy 3:14-15*

Peter said of the church:

> *But you are a chosen race, a royal priesthood, a holy nation, a people for his own possession, that you may proclaim the excellencies of him who called you out of darkness into his marvelous light. ~ 1 Peter 2:9*

The church is the household of God, the pillar and buttress of the truth. We are chosen, royal and holy. We have a purpose which is to proclaim the excellencies of Christ. These terms are not just platitudes. What a joyful wonder it is to be part of a church that loves the Lord and His word.

So… to church or not to church?

I will “church,” and do so with God’s word as the foundation and Jesus as the focus.

I hope you will too.

Chapter Five

What is happening?

This may be the longest chapter... it might be the shortest. But have you, like me, asked the question – what in the world is happening?

We currently live in a world gone mad.

It won't always be this way, for someday God will fulfill His redemptive plan and purge this world of sin. Until that time, we live in this dystopian world filled with myopic men and women who cannot see the world is steeped in a moral and ethical quagmire.

As I write this chapter, there is an elevated hostility in the world. More than just the usual aggression between nations and general unrest of various populations, the world has stepped into a greater condition of violence and anger.

Fires have ravaged communities in major cities, not through natural disasters but through the furious and vicious outbursts of people. Riotous individuals stormed the Capital building in Washington D.C. and wreaked havoc. Rancorous people have turned to striking against their neighbors for slights they see happening from other quarters. It's as if within the cities of our nation demilitarized zones have been created.

The "cancel culture" has moved to silence opposing voices. The former president was cut from his social media, Christians have faced increasing marginalization, and conservative voices are shouted down or silenced in the marketplace of ideas.

And if that wasn't enough... ideology worship has become the religion of the day.

Lest I forget, there's the pandemic that is currently reaching epic proportions.

Wait, really?

I'm not going to render here the entirety of what I've read concerning this pandemic, but suffice it to say it is the least "pandemicky" pandemic I've ever read about. I don't minimize the suffering that many have gone through nor dismiss the sorrow that has happened with the loss of life, for there were many who did lose the battle against the coronavirus. And, there are millions who lose the battle against cancers, heart diseases, blood disorders, and a multitude of other nefarious illnesses that destroy lives.

Death has happened, but death has always happened from the days of Adam and Eve. It doesn't lessen the pain, but it must bring us to face the reality that in this world we have a fleeting existence compared to the truth of eternity. Somewhere, in some way, you will live forever in some state of being – either in glory with Christ Jesus or in the perdition of God's forever wrath.

One reality this latest pandemic illuminated is the fractured nature of society. Strife and division has reared its ugly head and caused people who once enjoyed fellowship and friendship to stand at odds because of their response to the crisis.

I've groaned under the constant barrage of arguments between wearing a mask to save others from a virus we may or may not have versus rejecting the mask because it is merely a means of governmental control.

And now a vaccine has been developed that is so controversial the government tries to bribe people to take it by means of various incentives. Some transportation companies won't allow travelers to board if they don't have what is colloquially called a "vaccine passport."

Other divides have occurred. The grand argument over what is called "critical race theory" has sent educational institutions over the edge with animosity and vitriolic arguments. A movement like "defund the police" has sent civilized society into the abyss of chaotic anarchy.

At every point in life it seems that division, strife, contention and conflict grows.

What is going on?

Again, I turn to the only source of truth I know is completely reliable. I can't trust the news – goodness knows they can't be trusted. So I go to God's word and ask the question of Him.

"Lord, what's happening?"

I look to God's word and realize that, from the moment sin entered into the experience of human nature, the battle of good versus evil has continued. The wicked will always hate the righteous. That is what is happening in the world.

Even from the days of Cain and Abel:

> *In the course of time Cain brought to the Lord an offering of the fruit of the ground, and Abel also brought of the firstborn of his flock and of their fat portions. And the Lord had regard for Abel and his offering, but for Cain and*

> *his offering he had no regard. So Cain was very angry, and his face fell. The Lord said to Cain, "Why are you angry, and why has your face fallen? If you do well, will you not be accepted? And if you do not do well, sin is crouching at the door. Its desire is contrary to you, but you must rule over it." Cain spoke to Abel his brother. And when they were in the field, Cain rose up against his brother Abel and killed him. ~ Genesis 4:3-8*

God refused Cain's offering for it was given with no real devotion or love for God. And yet, with great compassion the Lord Almighty gives guidance to Cain and a warning against the sin that was "crouching at his door." All Cain needed to do was repent and leave off his self-centered approach to God. Humility and the fear of the Lord is what God is calling upon all mankind to embrace.

Listen to the words of Solomon from Proverbs:

> *The fear of the Lord is instruction in wisdom, and humility comes before honor. ~ Proverbs 15:33*

Consider the words from Isaiah:

> *For thus said the Lord God, the Holy One of Israel, "In returning [repentance] and rest you shall be saved; in quietness and in trust shall be your strength." But you were unwilling. ~ Isaiah 30:15*

What was Cain's response?

He did the same thing that the wicked have done throughout the ages and even in our modern era. The wicked strike out against the righteous.

Who are the righteous?

The righteous are those who fear the Lord and turn away from evil, those who have abandoned selfish and self-centered living and surrendered to the salvation of the Lord Jesus Christ. The righteous are those who love God more than themselves and will do as Abel did, show that love through genuine affection toward Him.

Consider the two offerings of those ancient brothers.

Cain brought "an offering." Okay. What's wrong with that? It was a sacrifice with no affection in it, no love for God. He brought what he wanted not what God required.

Compare it to Abel's offering when the second brother brought "the firstborn of his flock and their fat portions." Abel brought the best of the best. He gave to God out of a heart of love and devotion, with strong desire to do more than what was expected. He wanted to express His love for God.

This same condition existed in the days of Malachi.

> *"A son honors his father, and a servant his master. If then I am a father, where is my honor? And if I am a master, where is my fear? says the Lord of hosts to you, O priests, who despise my name. But you say, 'How have we despised your name?' By offering polluted food upon my altar. But you say, 'How have we polluted you?' By saying that the Lord's table may be despised. When you offer blind animals in sacrifice, is that not evil? And when you offer those that are lame or sick, is that not evil? Present that to your governor; will he accept you or show you favor? says the Lord of hosts." ~ Malachi 1:6-8*

The great calamity during the days of Malachi was a half-hearted devotion and worship of God. God is never honored with such meaningless sacrifice.

Then I find my eyes fixed upon the prophet Isaiah, chapter 59 to be exact. Can I encourage you to go and read that chapter?

Here is a statement from that text:

> *Justice is turned back, and righteousness stands far away; for truth has stumbled in the public squares, and uprightness cannot enter. Truth is lacking, and he who departs from evil makes himself a prey. ~ Isaiah 59:14-15*

Why do I point out the two passages above? Because, this is what we are experiencing in our world today. Meaningless worship that is centered on self and a vacuum of truth in the public conversations of our world has created a catastrophic disintegration of society.

I read further and find that the book of Romans, chapter one, is unfolding right before my eyes. Consider the final words of that chapter and ask yourself if this doesn't describe the condition of our world.

> *And since they did not see fit to acknowledge God, God gave them up to a debased mind to do what ought not to be done. They were filled with all manner of unrighteousness, evil, covetousness, malice. They are full of envy, murder, strife, deceit, maliciousness. They are gossips, slanderers, haters of God, insolent, haughty, boastful, inventors of evil, disobedient to parents, foolish, faithless, heartless, ruthless. Though they know God's righteous decree that*

> *those who practice such things deserve to die, they not only do them but give approval to those who practice them. ~ Romans 1:28-32*

This world (and my nation in particular) has fallen into such darkness of sin that it's a wonder God has withheld His day of wrath so long. Another prophet, Jeremiah, seemed to speak to this trend as well.

> *And you shall say to them, 'This is the nation that did not obey the voice of the Lord their God, and did not accept discipline; truth has perished; it is cut off from their lips." ~ Jeremiah 7:28*

Have you felt, perhaps like I've felt, that the situation is just WAY TOO BIG to face? What am I supposed to do? How in the world can I possibly make an impact on an avalanche when all I am capable of doing is picking up pebbles? These are some of the questions I've asked myself.

I preach the truth, but truth has stumbled in public and has perished in the hearts of man. I cry out against the storm and fight like a madman to battle against the encroaching chaos but my strength is slight and the situation massive.

Loved ones in my life have joined in the attack against the truth and I weep for their souls, knowing that they are truly on the losing side. They must come to Christ.

I feel like perhaps I understand the apostles a bit more when they were in a storm and Jesus was sleeping:

> *On that day, when evening had come, he said to them, "Let us go across to the other side." And leaving the crowd, they took him with them in the boat, just as he was. And other boats were with*

> *him. And a great windstorm arose, and the waves were breaking into the boat, so that the boat was already filling. But he was in the stern, asleep on the cushion. And they woke him and said to him, "Teacher, do you not care that we are perishing?" And he awoke and rebuked the wind and said to the sea, "Peace! Be still!" And the wind ceased, and there was a great calm. He said to them, "Why are you so afraid? Have you still no faith?" And they were filled with great fear and said to one another, "Who then is this, that even the wind and the sea obey him?" ~ Mark 4:35-41*

The waves of the sea of unrighteousness are crashing into the boat and I'm battling against it. Then, when I look, it seems that Jesus is completely unaware of what is happening – He's sleeping. But, like those apostles, I need to go to Jesus and tell Him my fear. Let Him know my terror in this current plight.

But when I do and Jesus acts in such a way that there is no mistaking it was His work which changed the situation, then I feel again like the apostles and I am "filled with great fear." Jesus, who can command the wind and the waves, can command all things and demand obedience from everything – including me.

Perhaps I'm asking the wrong question this time. "What's happening in the world?" might not be what I need to ask.

Maybe I need to ask, instead: "Lord, what will you have me do?"

I must ask that question no matter what is happening in the world. I cannot fix society. I cannot stop the winds and waves from beating against the boat. But I can offer to God my heart and my life, and lay before

Him the acceptable sacrifices of humble and contrite heart.

Two passages before we end this chapter:

> *The sacrifices of God are a broken spirit; a broken and contrite heart, O God, you will not despise. ~ Psalm 51:7*

And...

> *For thus says the One who is high and lifted up, who inhabits eternity, whose name is Holy: "I dwell in the high and holy place, and also with him who is of a contrite and lowly spirit, to revive the spirit of the lowly, and to revive the heart of the contrite. ~ Isaiah 57:15*

Whatever is happening in the world, let us seek the Lord and trust in our God, resting ever in His sovereign plan.

Chapter Six

Why Do I Pray?

In truth, the answer is simple.

I pray because I love the Lord Jesus Christ.

There is a tremendous longing in my heart, a soul-deep desperation that draws me ever into communication – even communion – with the Lord.

I can't begin to fathom a relationship with the Lord, or any relationship for that matter, that does not have at its core a well-trodden path of conversation. Could you imagine a husband and wife, having been married for any length of time, who never really talked with each other? I've actually seen it. I knew a husband and wife who sat across from each other in the living room of their home and the only thing that ever spoke with them was the television.

Who do you think they actually had a relationship with? That's right: the TV.

Silence is a deafening reality in a relationship, and it screams out the facts that such a relationship is broken. In fact, one of the methods we use to show our anger toward another is literally called the "silent treatment."

Prayer is supposed to be that deep and abiding communication you have with the Lord. It stands to reason, then, that silence between you and the Lord Jesus is a sure sign that your fellowship with Him is fractured, or worse, there might not be a real relationship with the Lord at all.

The Bible is rich with the importance of prayer. The call of God to commune with Him in prayer is replete throughout the Scriptures. If you read much of the book of Psalms, they are the heart-cry prayers of the authors.

> *On the day I called, you answered me; my strength of soul you increased. ~ Psalm 138:3*

Let's be honest, many people have transformed prayer into a formulaic and even ritualistic religious expression that has little real relationship value to it at all. We tack on the phrase, "in Jesus' name, amen" and hope that it sends our prayers like an important memo to the desk of the Almighty.

I began to think about this some years ago. What if we talked with our spouses the way we talk with the Lord. Could you imagine the looks on their faces when we step up to them and begin our conversation with, "Dear (spouse's name), I need you to purchase laundry soap and dryer sheets. Thank you for making dinner last night. You are an amazing spouse. I love you. In marriages' name, amen."

Yes, I know that it's silly. Though, perhaps for some it might be the best they've ever heard from their husband or wife.

But, like I said, years ago as I thought about this I began to consider how much I love to communicate with my wife. We could while away the nights in conversation about deep things or silly things, about family and spiritual truths. Truly we talk about everything.

Then it hit me.

Do I talk with the Lord with the same openness, with the same deep communion, as I talk with my wife?

And the startling answer to that question was: no. I didn't talk with the Lord in the same openness. I fell into the formulaic trap that made my "prayer life" something of a rote ritual that failed to bring me into a depth of relationship with Him.

So I took to reading books on how to have a powerful prayer life, steps to increasing your prayers, how to guarantee answers to prayers – and the list would go on and on. However, all of those books seemed more about how to get more out of God than grow closer to Him. It was more about the "stuff" down here and making God respond rather than seeking a deeper and more intimate fellowship with the Savior.

The disciples asked a very simple and profound question.

"Teach us to pray." ~ Luke 11:1

The answer Jesus gave was a review of the teaching He gave in the Sermon on the Mount:

> *"And when you pray, you must not be like the hypocrites. For they love to stand and pray in the synagogues and at the street corners, that they may be seen by others. Truly, I say to you, they have received their reward. But when you pray, go into your room and shut the door and pray to your Father who is in secret. And your Father who sees in secret will reward you. "And when you pray, do not heap up empty phrases as the Gentiles do, for they think that they will be heard for their many words. Do not be*

like them, for your Father knows what you need before you ask him. Pray then like this: Our Father in heaven, hallowed be your name. Your kingdom come, your will be done, on earth as it is in heaven. Give us this day our daily bread, and forgive us our debts, as we also have forgiven our debtors. And lead us not into temptation, but deliver us from evil. For if you forgive others their trespasses, your heavenly Father will also forgive you, but if you do not forgive others their trespasses, neither will your Father forgive your trespasses." ~ Matthew 6:5-15

I was tired of being "like the hypocrites" and merely reciting formula prayers that were little more than routine religious exercises. I wanted to pray in relationship, to communicate with the Father because I love Him.

Right now as I write this portion, in the church where I serve as pastor, we are holding a twelve hour prayer event. Many have come through, praying for the various ministries and needs that have been expressed. We've seen God answer prayer, and respond to the requests of His saints.

But that is not the first and foremost reason why I pray, to get answers. I pray because I want to get God. That is, to get to know God in all His infinite beauty and glorious holiness. I long to stand before His throne in celebration and to experience His magnificent presence. I crave the time I'm alone with the Lord, and often that is when I'm taking a walk (even on the golf course). I talk out loud and open my heart to all that He might whisper to me from His word.

It is the craving of fellowship, even of friendship. Jesus Himself called us friends who obey His word (John 15:14). And this is my great desire and delight, to experience fellowship with the Lord Jesus. Consider what He promises to those who trust Him:

> *"Whoever has my commandments and keeps them, he it is who loves me. And he who loves me will be loved by my Father, and I will love him and manifest myself to him." Judas (not Iscariot) said to him, "Lord, how is it that you will manifest yourself to us, and not to the world?" Jesus answered him, "If anyone loves me, he will keep my word, and my Father will love him, and we will come to him and make our home with him. Whoever does not love me does not keep my words. And the word that you hear is not mine but the Father's who sent me." ~ John 14:21-24*

Imagine that! Being so loved by God and in fellowship with Christ it is as if God sets up residence in our hearts. He makes His home with us and abides in loving fellowship with all who love Him and keep His commands. This is the first, best reason to pray—because God dwells with us. It is rather rude to not talk with someone who does.

I also pray because there are works of God that happen when I pray. God wants us to pray so He can put His power and glory on display through our lives.

> *Call to me and I will answer you,*
> *and will tell you great and hidden*
> *things that you have not known.*
> *~ Jeremiah 33:3*

It is not that I have some great spiritual presence or influence upon the heart of God. Just the opposite! God has a great and spiritual influence upon my heart. We don't pray for that which we desire but for that which God desires.

Again, in the Gospel of John, we discover that God is glorified when He responds to our prayers.

> *"If you abide in me, and my words abide in you, ask whatever you wish, and it will be done for you. By this my Father is glorified, that you bear much fruit and so prove to be my disciples."*
> *~ John 15:7-8*

Our "fruitfulness" is tied to our praying, and our praying is tied to the Word of God. If the Word of God abides in you, what kind of prayers do you think will be coming from you? To abide is to do more than take up space, it is to have preferential position. We "abide" in Christ, and that gives us a position of communion with Him. His word abides in us and that gives it a preferential situation in us. Thus, when you pray it is glorifying to God because He will answer the prayers that are born out of our fellowship with Jesus.

Paul had tremendous confidence in the prayers of God's people as he said in Philippians 1:19, "for I know that through your prayers and the help of the Spirit of Jesus Christ this will turn out for my deliverance."

Consider the role of prayer when Peter was released from prison in the book of Acts.

> *So Peter was kept in prison, but earnest prayer for him was made to God by the church. Now when Herod was about to bring him out, on that very night, Peter was sleeping between two soldiers, bound with two chains, and sentries before the door were guarding the prison. And behold, an angel of the Lord stood next to him, and a light shone in the cell. He struck Peter on the side and*

> *woke him, saying "Get up quickly." And the chains fell off his hands. ~ Acts 12:5-7*

James talks about the effective power of prayer and used Elijah as the example for the church to be faithful and fervent in their prayers:

> *Elijah was a man with a nature like ours, and he prayed fervently that it might not rain, and for three years and six months it did not rain on the earth. Then he prayed again, and heaven gave rain, and the earth bore its fruit. ~ James 5:17-18*

Why do I pray? You might as well ask me why I breathe. I pray, because I have no spiritual life without it.

Chapter Seven

Not Afraid to Die

That might sound like a strange title to a chapter, and as I write this chapter the world is still in the grip of the Covid-19 dilemma. But it's true... I'm not afraid to die.

Fear is a powerful thing, my friends. And the fear of death is probably the most controlling fear in life.

It's hard for people to fathom why someone might not be afraid to die. They may think that such a person is deluded or deranged in some fashion. Perhaps they may take that statement to mean the person is suicidal. Though, in light of that last one, I don't think suicidal people are afraid to die, they're afraid to live (but that's another chapter).

Before I go into the reasons why death doesn't frighten me, let's take a look at some other things related to it.

I think there is a great illusion going around wherein people are made to believe that the longer they live, the better. Somehow, we've made longevity the mark of winning at life. The world celebrates the person who made it over 100 years old as if they are a "superstar" or they "won the game!"

Many years ago, I sat at the bedside of a man who was at least that old. Let me tell you the story.

One afternoon, at the church where I served, I received a phone call from a pair of sisters who were greatly troubled in their hearts because their father lay in a hospital and he was very ill. They pleaded with me to go and pray with him, offer some comfort and sit with him for a moment of spiritual discussion.

So, I went.

When I arrived at the hospital, admittedly, I was expecting to see a pair of thirty-something women who fretted for their father. I entered the waiting room and found the two sisters sitting together with grief-stricken tears running down their cheeks. They were both over eighty years old.

Here I was, sitting with these two women and me being only in my early thirties. Yet their grief was palpable. “Please pray,” they said, “that our father would recover.” I offered what comfort I could to them and agreed to pray with their father. Departing the waiting room, I walked down the hushed hallway to find their father.

When I found him he was lying in bed, wracked with pain, bent from arthritis, unable to roll over, skeletal thin. He was over 100 years old.

He could barely talk, though his eyes told me that he understood me as I spoke with him. Then, I asked him a question: “are you ready to meet Jesus?”

Oh the smile that creased the old man’s face glowed with anticipation. He loved the Lord and served our Father in heaven most of his life.

Then I said to him, “Your daughters have asked me to pray with you, that God will keep you going.” With a careful breath, I asked, "Do you want me to pray that God take you home tonight?"

Tears trickled down his cheek and with a soft and whispered voice he said, "Please do."

So I prayed. "Oh Father, your servant is tired and worn. In your grace, please bring him home this very night." Then, after meeting with the daughters one last time, I departed.

I received the call the next day. He had died in the night.

His daughters came to my office a couple days later and with great tears in their eyes, they lamented strongly saying, "Oh, he went too soon!"

I was struck dumb with that statement. How long did they want him to remain? Stuck in a broken body, wracked with pain and limited in existence, yet the sisters struggled to embrace the reality that death will come.

I was told once that "death is just a part of the natural process of life."

I don't agree.

If death were the "natural process" then why do we fear it so much? Why do so many people run from the possibility that it might catch them off guard? Why did two eighty-year-old sisters want me to pray that their 100+ year old father get healed?

Sure, God could have healed him. The Lord could have restored that man of over a century into the pristine image of his twenty-year-old self and leave flabbergasted two octogenarian sisters.

But death is not the "natural process." Death is the catastrophic judgment of God against sin and it goes against the very sense of life that God has instilled into our hearts. Ecclesiastes 3:11 tells us that God "has put eternity into man's heart."

Yet God also said:

> *Behold, all souls are mine; the soul of the father as well as the soul of the son is mine: the soul who sins shall die. ~ Ezekiel 18:4*

So I wonder, when we see death does the notion hit us: this is the judgment of God? When we go to a funeral are we overwhelmed with the awareness that the body of flesh embalmed is the final outcome of being a sinner? Could this be why people try to "dodge the bullet" of the encroaching timestamp of life? Is there a sense in which people intuitively know that death is the manifestation of God's judgment?

So we have two realities working against each other in our own mentality: we are built for eternity, yet everyone will die.

But in reality, what is "death?"

Death is, ultimately, separation. When a person dies in the flesh, that is, in this world, they are separated from all those who remain in this world. You and I can't reach them from earth, or cross the threshold to where they are without ourselves dying too. At the time of this writing, my own father has been gone from this world for almost two decades. I cannot reach him... he cannot reach me. Death has separated us.

But I don't think that physical death is at the heart of why people are afraid to die. The loss of life, the disintegration of purpose, vitality and meaning all come into play for those who do not have an eternal view. But, perhaps (and this is speculation on my part), there is something deeper in the mind of man than just the loss of physical life. Perhaps somewhere, hidden in the shadows of our thinking, we know God's judgment is coming.

In the book of Hebrews we are reminded that it is appointed for man, after death, to face the judgment of God.

> *And just as it is appointed for man to die once, and after that comes judgment. ~ Hebrews 9:27*

And so people run from death. They try to hide from it, thwart it, control it and evade it as long as possible because this may be the only real life they have – at least for those without hope of eternity.

Perhaps that is why people feel so victorious when someone has lived a long time on this earth. They were able to avoid the judgment of God for as long as possible. Minor victories are all they have who have no hope beyond death.

But how permanent is physical death? Consider some of these texts:

> *And she said to Elijah, "What have you against me, O man of God? You have come to me to bring my sin to remembrance and to cause the death of my son!"*

And he said to her, "Give me your son." And he took him from her arms and carried him up into the upper chamber where he lodged, and laid him on his own bed. And he cried to the Lord, "O Lord my God, have you brought calamity even upon the widow with whom I sojourn, by killing her son?" Then he stretched himself upon the child three times and cried to the Lord, "O Lord my God, let this child's life come into him again." And the Lord listened to the voice of Elijah. And the life of the child came into him again, and he revived. ~ 1 Kings 17:18-22

And as a man was being buried, behold, a marauding band was seen and the man was thrown into the grave of Elisha, and as soon as the man touched the

> *bones of Elisha, he revived and stood on his feet. ~ 2 Kings 13:21*
>
> *Taking her by the hand he said to her, "Talitha cumi," which means, "Little girl, I say to you, arise." And immediately the girl got up and began walking (for she was twelve years of age), and they were immediately overcome with amazement. ~ Mark 5:41-42*
>
> *When he had said these things, he cried out with a loud voice, "Lazarus, come out." The man who had died came out, his hands and feet bound with linen strips, and his face wrapped with a cloth. Jesus said to them, "Unbind him, and let him go." ~ John 11:43-44*

There are other places in the Scriptures where you would find that the physical death of a person was overcome by the power of God. Even our Lord Jesus conquered death when He rose Himself from the grave.

Physical death is not the end. It is the temporary separation that is experienced by all people on this earth.

Spiritual death is the great thing to fear.

And, I'm not afraid to die.

You may ask, why? I'm glad you asked.

Because: the death of a person is the result of the judgment of God. It is sin that brings death because God must punish all sin. And God provided redemption for all who believe.

Believe what?

Believe on the Lord Jesus Christ, His substitutionary atonement paid upon the cross. He bore God's judgment and wrath, the punishment that we deserved. Jesus Christ, the Righteous One, suffered the death we earned. He endured the full wrath of God so that all who believe on Him might not perish but have everlasting life.

Consider the words of Jesus:

> *"I am the resurrection and the life. Whoever believes in me, though he die, yet shall he live, and everyone who lives and believes in me shall never die. Do you believe this?" ~ John 11:25-26*

Paul encouraged the church with these words:

> *For God has not destined us for wrath, but to obtain salvation through our Lord Jesus Christ, who died for us so that whether we are awake or asleep we might live with him. Therefore encourage one another and build one another up, just as you are doing. ~ 1 Thessalonians 5:9-11*

People are controlled by their fear of death. They run from it, hide from it, and do all they can to delay it for the simple fact they have no assurance that what will come next is anything other than the wrath of God. Because of this fear of death, all of mankind has been under the enslavement of the enemy of God.

But for those who have received God's mercy and grace, those who know the salvation of the Lord Jesus Christ, these people are set free from such bondage.

So, I'm not afraid to die. Jesus took my death. He endured my punishment. He loved me so much that He willingly suffered the wrath of God so that I could be set free from the fear of death. Even as the Scripture says:

> *Since therefore the children share in flesh and blood, he himself likewise partook of the same things, that through death he*

> *might destroy the one who has the power of death, that is, the devil, and deliver all those who through fear of death were subject to lifelong slavery. ~ Hebrews 2:14-15*

If I did not have faith in Christ, I would be living in fear as much of the world is today. I would strive to find every advantage that would provide me the longest life possible, delaying the inevitable until the last possible moment.

But death is inevitable. Everyone will taste its bitter drink. But for those who believe in Christ for salvation, who have run to the only hope given by the only One who could fulfill that hope, the Lord Jesus, there is now no need to fear.

Consider these words:

> *When the perishable puts on the imperishable, and the mortal puts*

on immortality, then shall come to pass the saying that is written: "Death is swallowed up in victory." ~ 1 Corinthians 15:54

Because of Jesus, I am not afraid to die.

Chapter Eight

Afraid to Live

I'm afraid of heights... but I've gone mountain climbing.

I'm afraid of the dark... but I've been spelunking.

I'm afraid of crowds... but I spend every Sunday in the fellowship of God's people.

In truth, there are times I feel like I'm afraid to live, but I push myself beyond the barrier of fear to engage my life in those things that I will either conquer or suffer. Does that mean I'm alive?

Is being truly alive just the sequential overcoming of various phobias until the time of termination? Life has to be more than just overcoming greater risks and compiling a better social media profile that displays myriad adventures along the way.

And, in truth, I've seen that very thing. People grasp upon one moment after another and post those moments to their favorite social network hoping to generate some semblance of being alive. They crave attention and seek affirmation that they have "lived." And when the world looks upon them and declares "oh what a life you have" they feel reassured and believe they are truly alive.

There are nearly a billion people on Facebook but still there are more than seven billion people in the world. What are those remaining six billion people doing? Are they missing out on life?

What does it mean to be alive?

Many, I believe, are afraid to answer that question. Why, you ask? Because being alive is far more than merely existing in this world. Being alive implies a reality, a purpose and reason for all that is and all that there is to come. When someone is truly alive that same someone begins to understand a remarkable truth: their existence is far more than just the momentary position of their mobilized molecules pandering to the whims and fancies of their imagination. Being alive means they have a purpose—and a responsibility to that purpose. There are eternal issues at play when someone finally comes alive.

That is why life for many is a fearful thing.

I'm not afraid of the challenges or the difficulties, those I've faced for most of my adulthood (and some of my childhood). But real life, the unmistakable pursuit of that which is larger than self, that scares me. And not only me, it scares everyone.

Let me explain why this is true of me.

Life scares me for a couple of reasons. First: who am I to say my life is of any value or has any purpose or destiny that is of such consequence it forces me to push through all obstacles until the final moment when it's over? Second, and perhaps the greater of the two fears, what if I get it wrong?

Let's begin by tackling the first reason: Who am I to say my life is of any value?

Maybe the problem lies in the reality that we all start off in life... dead.

What!? That's a bold statement and seemingly incongruous to the fact that people are walking around breathing and eating. It boggles the mind to think that people are merely ambulatory corpses on a dusty road from the cradle to the grave. After all, the world doesn't look like a zombie apocalypse movie.

And yet, what does the Bible say?

> *And you were dead in the trespasses and sins. ~ Ephesians 2:1*

Think about it for just a moment. The frantic, even frenetic pursuit of the multitudes of people in this world, with the hope of finding something that will bring value and meaning to their ambulation across this planet, is, in essence the dead trying to find life. It is, as the book of Ecclesiastes says, a "chasing after the wind."

> *And I applied my heart to seek and to search out by wisdom all that is done under heaven. It is an unhappy business that God has given to the children of man to be busy with. I have seen everything that is done under the sun, and behold, all is vanity and a striving after wind. ~ Ecclesiastes 1:13-14*

This striving of humanity does not contain the seed of life but of death. In contrast to the proverbial "Midas touch," the unmitigated effect of anything done by this fallen world is not precious gold which has lasting and intrinsic value, but painful grief that leaves a fallen world still fallen.

Remember what James said:

But each person is tempted when he is lured and enticed by his own desire. Then desire when it has conceived gives birth to sin, and sin when it is fully grown brings forth death. ~ James 1:14-15

Consider this: We've advanced in technology, but the depravity of man continues. We've expedited social sciences and yet the human race is more fractured than ever. We've made and modified laws and yet violence and criminals abound. In all aspects of our effort to find real life and become "alive" we discover that death is still at work in everything.

And then I look at myself. I can sympathize with the writer of Ecclesiastes.

Though I've not had the wherewithal to embark on the variety of experiences he did, I can honestly say that the expenditure of effort I've given to try and discover on my own what it means to be "alive" has ended in fruitless vines. Oh, there have been some grand adventures that have taken me to places I enjoyed. There have been some amazing experiences that I have locked away in the vaults of memory. But, as I look back, even now, I ask a simple question: what value did I add to anything by pursuing only that which I desired? What will carry on after me, and on into eternity, of those things I tried to do to please myself? In the end, it is merely a chasing after the wind.

So, from that depressive view, I wonder if anything of me matters at all. I'm afraid to live because to live only for myself ultimately ends in death.

And that brings me to the second reason I'm afraid to live – and perhaps actually the primary reason – what if I get it wrong?

Have you ever been there, afraid to do something for fear that you will get it wrong? Of course you have. Everyone has unless they are some grand narcissist who cannot fathom their own failings. But for many, including myself, the fear of failure and the insecurity of uncertainty weigh heavily upon the pursuit of life.

Consider Moses for a moment. He was called upon by God to do a work of such importance that it would change the course of all mankind. He was tasked with the deliverance of God's people from the clutches of Pharaoh. What was his response? Did Moses rise up with great aplomb and make his way to Egypt with unwavering determination? No. In fact, on five separate occasions he tried to find a reason to not be tasked with this calling.

So great were his objections to the task that he asked God to send another.

> *But Moses said to the Lord, "Oh, my Lord, I am not eloquent, either in the past or since you have spoken to your servant, but I am*

> *slow of speech and of tongue." Then the Lord said to him, "Who has made man's mouth? Who makes him mute, or deaf, or seeing, or blind? Is it not I, the Lord? Now therefore go, and I will be with your mouth and teach you what you shall speak." But he said, "Oh, my Lord, please send someone else." ~ Exodus 4:10-13*

I can understand this.

I look at my own life and marvel that God can use me for anything. The truth of the matter is, it's not my life that is of use – it's the life of Christ in me.

In all the objections Moses offered, the Father in heaven rebuffed them all. God Almighty cared very little for Moses' infirmity, insecurity or inadequacy. In fact, let me say it this way: there is not one aspect of the fallen human condition that can add even a drop of life to the pursuit of it. Any vain belief that we can accomplish life without the Lord will ultimately end in eternal failure.

God didn't tell Moses to go to Pharaoh and deliver the nation of Israel on his own. He told Moses, "I will be with you" (Exodus 3:12). None of us, not one single person in all the earth, can accomplish life without the Author of life providing it.

So in light of my two main objections (that I am not worthy and that I might get it wrong) the truth of the matter is this: I'm not and I would—if I were to try on my own.

And so I am afraid to live. But this is true only when I try to live without Christ Jesus as the source and sustaining power of my life.

Think about these two passages of Scripture:

In him was life, and the life was the light of men. ~ John 1:4

"The thief comes only to steal and kill and destroy. I came that they may have life and have it abundantly." ~ John 10:10

To be alive, my friends, is to have Jesus Christ as Savior and to follow Him as Lord. He does not come simply to give you comfort and a promise of heaven.

He came to make dead people live and to make that life an experience of abundance. Before you imagine a tangent that I'm not headed down, this is not the abundance of selfish pursuits or worldly endeavors that only feed the ego and satisfy carnal desires, but an abundance of life that blossoms with eternal significance and rich with everlasting joy.

Jesus is the light of life, and in Him is that life. There is, truly, no life outside of Him.

Without Christ we don't breathe, we don't see, we don't think. Simply put: we don't have life.

Thus, any pursuit of life outside of knowing and following Christ will always end in eternal tragedy. Even if during the entire journey along the paths of this world you find that every road is pleasant and every way is prosperous, in the end if it is outside of Christ, there is no life in it. You should be afraid to live outside of Jesus. And, in fact, you cannot live outside of Him, though many people think they do.

Consider the question Jesus posed:

> *"For whoever would save his life will lose it, but whoever loses his life for my sake will find it. For what will it profit a man if he gains the whole world and forfeits his soul? Or what shall a man give in return for his soul?" ~ Matthew 16:25-26*

It seems like a simple truth: if you lose your soul, you've lost everything! Imagine that you have gained all the wealth of all the world of all time and then you live to 100 years old. Is that worth forfeiting eternity? You will live forever somewhere; your soul – that is, the very eternal nature of you – is going to survive your corporeal existence. And if life is eternal, it is imperative that we chose to live it with eternity in mind.

In His prayer, the Lord Jesus made this declaration:

> *"And this is eternal life, that they know you, the only true God, and Jesus Christ whom you have sent." ~ John 17:3*

So, yes, I am afraid to live – but only when I don't live for and with the Lord Jesus Christ. To live outside of Him is to merely exist, no matter how prosperous or adventurous it is.

The Apostle Paul recognized this reality when he told the Philippians how he viewed his life.

> *For to me to live is Christ, and to die is gain. If I am to live in the flesh, that means fruitful labor for me. Yet which I shall choose I cannot tell. I am hard pressed between the two. My desire is to depart and be with Christ, for that is far better. But to remain in the flesh is more necessary on your account. ~ Philippians 1:21-24*

Oh, my friends, let me encourage you to lose yourself in Christ and discover a life far more alive than you have ever known. The temporary adventures are enjoyable, and the baubles and trinkets of this world sparkle for a time. But don't let those become the only aspirations of your life.

Pursue Jesus Christ. Serve Him and you will discover that there is a life awaiting you that is rich with being alive.

Chapter Nine
Why Do I Care?

I have spent a lot of my time worried, fretting over the opinions of many people in my life. Why do I care?

I think one of the most debilitating realities of my life has been the hope that somehow I would be admired or considered worthy of attention. What a waste. Admired by whom? Are the crowds of this world remotely worth the energy it takes to fret over their lack of attention? Multitudes in this fallen human experience are often those that dive into the cesspools of sin and carouse with the powerful of our day—the "superstars" of our current generation. Those who get the most attention are often those who have made some horrendous splash, like a belly-flop in the shallow end of the culture pool.

As I write this chapter, the media is focused on a tragic circumstance that happened to the iconic golfer, Tiger Woods. He had a horrifying accident that required surgeries and made the headlines of every major news outlet. As terrible as that is, other people had accidents that same day. Five years ago (at the time of this writing), I was in a roll-over collision when a drunk driver crashed into my SUV and forced me off the road where I flipped four times and ended my drive upside-down on the opposite side of the highway.

It didn't make the news. I didn't get a headline.

So, then, why does this one person get such headlines? Because our society has elevated him to a status of superstar and thus his life takes on a whole different paradigm. Maybe he's always wanted to be a superstar. Perhaps he hates the entire experience! I don't know. I do hope and pray that he gets better, and at the time I'm writing this Mr. Woods is still hospitalized. It is a tragedy, and I've spent some time in prayer for him.

As I think back to my days growing up, during high school, I always stood envious of those who could attract a crowd.

Even more than that, I was envious of those who seemed unaffected by the "group-think" mentality and simply went their way no matter if anyone joined them or not. I wondered how they were able to separate themselves from the gripping anxiety that hounded me – the need to be noticed.

I grew up feeling practically invisible. I hated that feeling.

It wasn't true, of course. I had a small bevy of friends with whom I hung around and enjoyed. But there were always those one or two individuals who, when they entered a room, drew everyone's attention. From my vantage point of the socially invisible, I believed everyone loved them. They attracted attention, not because they performed antics on a continual basis but simply for being around.

I tried. I attempted to position myself into situations so others might notice me. I undertook to endear myself to those I thought were the attention getters. I hoped that if I could simply fall into the right circles then, finally, my life would blossom in the light of that spectacle.

I was so very wrong.

Once, while serving in the military, I roomed with a good friend and fellow Christian. He was one of those whom I just described. He was always "wanted." The phone would ring and several Christian friends of ours would throw a get-together and he got the invite... not me. Sometimes I would go with him only to watch as the swirling groups of people gathered around each other in various cliques while I sat drinking a soda on the sidelines.

One night, as he was preparing to venture out to another invite, I asked him what was wrong with me. His answer was rather startling.

"Michael," he said, "when you show up, everyone knows that eventually it's going to become a bible study. You're a good man... you're just not that fun."

And that seemed to settle it for him as he walked out the door.

But that didn't settle it for me. For years I was nagged with the unsettling belief that the crowds of humanity that I occasionally frequented never truly noticed that I was around. Even now, I'm pricked in my heart with the notion that if I were to vanish from my current place, the empty space I leave behind may lay vacant for lack of anyone's awareness that I'd left it. I longed for either the charisma to attract a crowd or, better yet, for the temperament to not care if there even was a crowd.

I know... but I'm not actually fishing for sympathy with these stories. There is a point to my sharing this with you, and it hinges on the question: why do I care?

Think about it. How many times do we go looking after we post something on our social media platforms to see who liked it, retweeted, gave it a thumbs up, added a heart or showed some mild interest in something we had said or done. Do we really care how many people noticed if we had spaghetti for dinner at the local café?

But we do care! Multitudes want to be noticed and that's why they post thousands of pictures and telegraph their every move so that someone, somewhere, will notice and make them momentarily "famous."

And society has adopted this new trend. We've moved from highlighting the "superstars" to magnifying a new title for those who fill the interest vacuums of our lives.

They are called: "influencers."

That's right. The great influencers of our day rocket to the stratosphere with their words, sayings, memes and comments. They post blogs and vlogs and host podcasts and webinars. And they are talked about... over and over again, they are talked about. These people don't toil in obscurity. They don't slog through the mire of the rank and file of the unnoticed. Nope. They are grand in stature and have more "likes" and "retweets" than anyone.

But why do I care? And why should I? The opinions and estimations of those I don't even know should not rise in consideration when it comes to the life I live. In fact, there should only be one place that I seek the affirmation of life—from God.

And this was the lesson God was teaching me.

Jesus said this to the Jewish rulers:

> *I do not receive glory from people. But I know that you do not have the love of God within you. I have*

> *come in my Father's name, and you do not receive me. If another comes in his own name, you will receive him. How can you believe, when you receive glory from one another and do not seek the glory that comes from the only God? ~ John 5:41-44*

Imagine... here is a group of Jewish leaders seeking glory "from one another" and missing the glory that comes from God! These were supposedly the spiritually minded. And yet, they were seeking the praise and adulation of their peers, the crowds, the "influencers" of their day all the while rejecting the idea that only God's praise was of any value.

You may recall in the book of Matthew, chapter twenty-five, the story of the master who gave various "talents" (which is a measure of currency in the days of Christ) to his servants. In the parable, Jesus reiterates the idea that the one person we must be faithful to is our Master in heaven. His praise should be our pursuit. His "well done" should be our ambition.

> *"And he who had received the five talents came forward, bringing five talents more, saying, 'Master, you delivered to me five talents; here, I have made five talents more.' His master said to him, 'Well done, good and faithful servant. You have been faithful over a little; I will set you over much. Enter into the joy of your master.' And he also who had the two talents came forward, saying, 'Master, you delivered to me two talents; here, I have made two talents more.' His master said to him, 'Well done, good and faithful servant. You have been faithful over a little; I will set you over much. Enter into the joy of*

your master.'" ~ Matthew 25:20-23.

What an invitation! "Enter into the joy of your master." Is there any better accolade or acceptance than knowing God Almighty is pleased and has invited you in to share His joy? All of the "influencers" of this world could not, with all their voices, measure up to that singular satisfaction: I am accepted by God and He is well pleased with me.

And then it hit me.

It was my ego, my pride that always sought after the applause of men. For, in truth, even as I read the Scriptures and know that God does say, "Well done," it is a heady experience to have the gathered crowds of humanity voicing their praise. It is a rush to my personal esteem when invited to speak at a conference or offer advice in a seminar. I am more convinced than ever there are pastors in heaven who receive far greater celebration because throughout their journey they faithfully toiled in obscurity and never sought the limelight of men.

Consider the Apostle's testimony to the church in Rome.

> *But a Jew is one inwardly, and circumcision is a matter of the heart, by the Spirit, not by the letter. His praise is not from man but from God. ~ Romans 2:29*

I won't go into the issue of physical circumcision. Suffice it to say, a Jewish man would never rise to any prominence without fulfilling the letter of the law. But God looks at the heart. Cutting away the shell of sinfulness is more precious to God than the outward fulfillment of religious requirements. Men may praise you for your external efforts to try and show off your religiosity. But when we seek our praise from God, it will outshine any external praise of man.

Remember what Paul said to the church in Corinth?

> *For consider your calling, brothers: not many of you were wise according to worldly standards, not many were powerful, not many were of noble birth. But God chose what is foolish in the world to shame the wise; God chose what is weak in the world to shame the strong; God chose what is low and despised in the world, even things that are not, to bring to nothing things that are. ~ 1 Corinthians 1:26-28*

The wise and powerful, the superstars and influencers are not often those God calls into His service. He chose the weak, the low and despised and the things that are not. But how often do we elevate the most prestigious and influential individuals? We see people in this world in a way that God does not, and it is time that our eyes adjust and start looking at life from God's point of view.

I began this chapter with the question: why do I care? Perhaps a better question is: what should I care about?

Jesus warned, if the world loves me it will love me as its own (John 15:19). I don't want that. What a remarkably empty life I would have at the end of my time in this world if all I ever lived for was the praise and love of men.

Paul told Timothy, "No soldier gets entangled in civilian pursuits, since his aim is to please the one who enlisted him" (2 Timothy 2:4). Jesus is the one who enlisted me. Getting entangled in the "civilian" pursuits of this world will only clog up my life with useless endeavors.

So I try, and fail on occasion, to limit my pursuit to the pleasing of One – the Lord Jesus. It is He who called me out of this world and into His kingdom. I long to hear Jesus say: "Well done, good and faithful servant."

That alone, will make everything worth it.

Chapter Ten

Finding Joy

"I'd just like to be happy."

That quote came to me from a friend who struggles along the journey of life. Yet that quote is often the hidden concern of the heart of those who face the reality of life.

Many, so very many people languish along the road of life with unending stress and pressure that seems to rob them of the circumstantial happiness pursued by humanity.

We work for the weekend... always laboring for the micro-moments that bring a sense of delight. But it doesn't last. There is nothing enduring about a moment of happiness. Like the mist that evaporates in the morning sun, we discover that circumstantial joy is a fleeting experience.

And yet, the majority of people around me are in hot pursuit of those fleeting moments. I must admit, even I still crave those experiential moments that bring short-term happiness.

This is where sin runs rampant through the heart of man. For the Scripture says that sin has its season of pleasure. Moses understood this—and rejected it.

> *By faith Moses, when he was grown up, refused to be called the son of Pharaoh's daughter, choosing rather to be mistreated with the people of God than to enjoy the fleeting pleasures of sin. He considered the reproach of Christ greater wealth than the treasures of Egypt, for he was looking to the reward. ~ Hebrews 11:24-26*

Rather than enjoying the “fleeting pleasures of sin,” Moses chose reproach and mistreatment, considering it to be of greater wealth than all the treasures of Egypt.

How many in our modern, pleasure-seeking culture would remotely agree with Moses? Self-love is the predominant pursuit. Within the “church-shopping” mindset, even some Christians have taken to the notion that their own fancies and desires are more important than a sacrificial life for Christ.

The book of Ecclesiastes is the testimony of a man who sought the vain pleasures of sin in hopes of discovering the meaning of life.

> *I said in my heart, "Come now, I will test you with pleasure; enjoy yourself." But behold, this also was vanity. I said of laughter, "It is mad," and of pleasure, "What use is it?" I searched with my heart how to cheer my body with wine—my heart still guiding me with wisdom—and how to lay hold on folly, till I might see what was good for the children of man to do under heaven during the few days of their life. ~ Ecclesiastes 2:1-3*

And again...

> *And whatever my eyes desired I did not keep from them. I kept my heart from no pleasure, for my heart found pleasure in all my*

> *toil, and this was my reward for all my toil. Then I considered all that my hands had done and the toil I had expended in doing it, and behold, all was vanity and a striving after wind, and there was nothing to be gained under the sun. ~ Ecclesiastes 2:10-11*

So the pursuit of pleasure is vanity and worldly wealth is of no value.

Still… like so many in this world… I just want to be happy.

So I have to ask the question: Is it wrong to pursue happiness?

I don't think so, provided that such a pursuit is in the right direction. Perhaps that's the general issue as to why it eludes so many and vanishes from sight like a rainbow in the sky. Most people are going the wrong way and chasing the wrong thing.

Selfishness is always wrong. And chasing after happiness in a selfish direction will, ultimately, be like chasing a drop of water in a river. Yet, the world around us is filled with the enticements of avarice. Pictures and trinkets and promises of pleasure swirl around our attentions in the hopes of instigating us to believe that they can satisfy our cravings for happiness.

So we test the waters.

We buy this gizmo; we purchase that gadget. We spend our hard-earned life on the fleeting pleasures of this world and hope we can make the joy last at least a day. We wear ourselves out in the rush of the hunt for the next moment of satisfaction.

And then it fades.

And, yes, I've had the same struggle as you. I've sought the fleeting and transient sense of happiness, hoping that the next delight will fill the cavernous need I started with: I just want to be happy.

Let me tell you what I learned along this very pot-hole infested road of life.

Beyond circumstantial happiness, true and lasting joy is never found in any pursuit that is selfish. I needed to look beyond myself, to abandon myself—even to die to myself—in order to finally learn that the greatest delight of life is found in sacrifice.

I know it sounds counterintuitive, but the greatest joy is found not in receiving but in giving. Consider what the Apostle Paul said in the book of Acts:

> *"In all things I have shown you that by working hard in this way we must help the weak and remember the words of the Lord Jesus, how he himself said, 'It is more blessed to give than to receive.'"* ~ *Acts 20:35*

Many think that if we are going to pursue those things that make us happy, then we must chase after selfish desires. Yet all the vacuous pleasures which the fallen heart of man might crave like money, power, fame and sex ultimately stand in contradiction to what truly brings actual fulfillment in life.

Ask yourself this question: after you've exhausted that particular fleeting pleasure in the pursuit of happiness, how long did the happiness last? My guess, not that long. Why would I know that? Because it's true of me as well. In seeking only temporary satisfactions I received only temporary happiness. And then, like all things in this world, it vanished like a vapor in a breeze.

Even seeming long-term pursuits like family and career, if they only have earthly considerations, will finally dissipate. Basically, nothing in this world lasts forever. Thus, to find lasting happiness and perpetual joy, it is incumbent upon all to seek for it in eternal truths.

So, we turn to Jesus.

In the Sermon on the Mount, the Savior offered this timely wisdom:

> *"Do not lay up for yourselves treasures on earth, where moth and rust destroy and where thieves break in and steal, but lay up for yourselves treasures in heaven, where neither moth nor rust destroys and where thieves do not break in and steal. For where your treasure is, there your heart will be also." ~ Matthew 6:19-21*

Everything in this temporary existence is nothing but what moth and rust and thieves have access. And if our hearts—that is, our pursuit of happiness—are centered upon those things they will soon be eaten, corrupted or stolen. Yet, if our treasures are laid up in heaven—that is, our lives are set for eternal pursuits—then we discover there is an abundance of joyful anticipation that carries us even along the course of this life. With our focus shifted, we discover an experience of joy in the present with the expectation of everlasting joy in eternity.

The Son of God offered us a life filled with joy. It is not the limited happiness of the world or of earthly circumstances, but a deep and abiding joy that flows from Him and fills our hearts. Consider His promise in the gospel of John:

> *"These things I have spoken to you, that my joy may be in you, and that your joy may be full." ~ John 15:11*

Have you ever asked this question: what was the joy of Jesus? He promised that "His joy" would be in us and "our joy" would be full. But what was "His joy?" Simply put, Jesus delighted to do the will of His Father. Consider what it says in Psalm 40.

> *I delight to do your will, O my God; your law is within my heart." ~ Psalm 40:8*

In this Messianic Psalm, it is clearly told that the delight of Jesus would be to do the will of His Father. And that is exactly what Jesus did. He lived in perfect obedience to God the Father, always with the fulfillment of God's will as His primary joy.

> *Looking to Jesus, the founder and perfecter of our faith, who for the joy that was set before him endured the cross, despising the shame, and is seated at the right hand of the throne of God. ~ Hebrews 12:2*

That great joy set before the Savior was the fulfillment of God's will by becoming the propitiation for sinful man. With anticipated joy set before Him, the Lord Jesus endured the scorn and shame and cruelty of the cross. And more than that, upon the cross, Jesus endured the full measure of God's wrath. With His eyes set upon the joy beyond the cross, He endured the cross and fulfilled the Father's will.

Again, in Hebrews 11:35b we see the response of faithful believers who had their mind set upon eternity. "Some were tortured, refusing to accept release, so that they might rise again to a better life." Though they might have been able to avoid torturous persecution, they refused the temporary relief for the eternal reward.

Jesus wants His joy to be in you and me. But for that to happen, it is important to have our concentration set upon Him.

Consider the experience of the first disciples.

For a brief time the disciples were separated from the Lord Jesus. During the three days of Christ's death, before His resurrection, the disciples were full of grief and anxiety. Many disciples fled into the darkness when the Roman soldiers took Jesus captive. Peter denied Jesus three times when given the opportunity to declare his faith and loyalty. Thomas didn't even believe he would look upon Jesus ever again.

When the disciples lost sight of Jesus they lost the joy that they had known for the previous three years. Jesus had warned them of this before it happened.

> *"So with you: Now is your time of grief, but I will see you again and you will rejoice, and no one will take away your joy." ~ John 16:22*

The promise of joy for the believer is found in the connected concentration we have upon our Lord Jesus. Let your mind stray from Him and you will find yourself lost in doubt and anxiety. Your joy will be lost when your concentration is not on Christ Jesus the Lord.

And consider that promise: "No one will take away your joy."

This truth becomes palpable when you take a look at the disciples in the early church as they faced the persecutions that fell upon them. They suffered and struggled against the onslaught of hatred from the world and yet, they rejoiced!

> *Then they left the presence of the council, rejoicing that they were counted worthy to suffer dishonor for the name. ~ Acts 5:41*

So if, like at the beginning of this chapter, you said (as I have) that you just want to be happy, then hear this from our Lord:

> *And he opened his mouth and taught them, saying: "Blessed are the poor in spirit, for theirs is the kingdom of heaven. Blessed are*

those who mourn, for they shall be comforted. Blessed are the meek, for they shall inherit the earth. Blessed are those who hunger and thirst for righteousness, for they shall be satisfied. Blessed are the merciful, for they shall receive mercy. Blessed are the pure in heart, for they shall see God. Blessed are the peacemakers, for they shall be called sons of God. Blessed are those who are persecuted for righteousness' sake, for theirs is the kingdom of heaven. ~ Matthew 5:2-10

The term "blessed" means, basically, "happy." Read the Scripture above once again and use the term "happy" in place of "blessed."

If you've ever said you just want to be happy, now you have the road set before you, which God has made for your happiness. You just have to be willing to walk it.

Chapter Eleven

To Those I Leave Behind

Someday, my friends, I will be gone. Whether I pass through the shadow of death or am snatched away by God to glory, I belong to Jesus Christ and He is my Savior and Lord. I will be with Him forever.

There will come a day when the wrath of God will fall upon the earth. As Scripture says:

> *For the wrath of God is revealed from heaven against all ungodliness and unrighteousness of men, who by their unrighteousness suppress the truth. ~ Romans 1:18*

When that happens, all who belong to Christ will be removed from the earth and spared those years of tribulation. For we read in 1 Thessalonians 5:9, "For God has not destined us for wrath, but to obtain salvation through our Lord Jesus Christ," and in Revelation 3:10, "Because you have kept my word about patient endurance, I will keep you from the hour of trial that is coming on the whole world, to try those who dwell on the earth."

If, in reading this letter, you discover that those who confessed Christ have all disappeared, then I beg you to find yourself a Bible and read the book of Revelation. It is all there, everything concerning the wrath of God. God spelled out all that will happen during that time and if you are willing, even now, to believe on the Lord Jesus Christ, you can be saved from God's final wrath.

For even in the midst of the final outpouring of God's anger against sin, He STILL offers salvation. There is a call for all who will to repent of sin and believe on the Lord Jesus for eternal salvation. Someday it will be too late.

If you're reading this and Christians are still around, please find one and ask: "What must I do to be saved?" God's word tells you. God's people know and if you can find a church that is grounded in the Word of God, then please go there and ask how you can be born again.

Jesus said it like this:

> *"Truly, truly, I say to you, unless one is born again he cannot see the kingdom of God.... For God so loved the world, that he gave his only Son, that whoever believes in him should not perish but have eternal life. For God did not send his Son into the world to condemn the world, but in order that the world might be saved through him. Whoever believes in him is not condemned, but whoever does not believe is condemned already, because he has not believed in the name of the only Son of God. And this is the judgment: the light has come into the world, and people loved the darkness rather than the light because their works were evil. For everyone who does wicked things hates the light and does*

> *not come to the light, lest his works should be exposed. But whoever does what is true comes to the light, so that it may be clearly seen that his works have been carried out in God." ~ John 3:3, 16-21*

If you have nowhere else to go, please reach out to me and I will tell you all that Jesus did in bearing the wrath of God and taking upon Himself the punishment for your sin and mine. He bore the entirety of God's eternal wrath that you should be saved. But you MUST believe and thus yield your life in faithfulness to the Lord Jesus Christ.

Paul speaks to this in the book of Romans:

> *For all have sinned and fall short of the glory of God, and are justified by his grace as a gift, through the redemption that is in Christ Jesus, whom God put forward as a propitiation by his*

> *blood, to be received by faith. This was to show God's righteousness, because in his divine forbearance he had passed over former sins. It was to show his righteousness at the present time, so that he might be just and the justifier of the one who has faith in Jesus.* ~ Romans 3:23-26

It is not about self-imposed religion. God condemns all religions that lead people to trusting in their own works for salvation. It's not about establishing a high moral code so you can try and prove you're good enough to be acceptable to God. No one is. All have sinned. Only Jesus lived without sin. The rest of us, all of humanity, must repent of sin. And the first and foremost sin that must be repented is unbelief.

Confess Jesus as Lord and believe that God raised Him from the dead. That is what we find again in God's word:

But what does it say? "The word is near you, in your mouth and in your heart" (that is, the word of faith that we proclaim); because, if you confess with your mouth that Jesus is Lord and believe in your heart that God raised him from the dead, you will be saved. For with the heart one believes and is justified, and with the mouth one confesses and is saved. For the Scripture says, "Everyone who believes in him will not be put to shame." For there is no distinction between Jew and Greek; for the same Lord is Lord of all, bestowing his riches on all who call on him. For "everyone who calls on the name of the Lord will be saved." ~ *Romans 10:8-13*

I implore you, believe on the Lord Jesus Christ and be saved! Your sins can be washed clean. Your life can be made new before God. He loves you and will redeem you if you come to Him by faith.

As I said at the beginning of this chapter, the day will come when I depart this world. Whether I pass through the shadow of death or am snatched away by God to glory, I belong to Jesus Christ. He is my Savior and Lord. I will be with Him forever. Do not let this day pass without knowing that you belong to Jesus Christ as well.

EPILOGUE

FOR KING AND CROWN

I sit here pondering how I want to conclude these brief conversations on the Christian life. In truth, I don't want to conclude. I hope these conversations will continue in your own heart as they do in mine. And I hope this little book will inspire you to dialogue with other believers around you in order that you might continue to grow and advance in your Christian walk.

Two passages of Scripture come to mind as I think on this.

> *Rather, speaking the truth in love, we are to grow up in every way into him who is the head, into Christ, from whom the whole body, joined and held together by every joint with which it is equipped, when each part is working properly, makes the body grow so that it builds itself up in love. ~ Ephesians 4:15-16*

And...

> *Then those who feared the Lord spoke with one another. The Lord paid attention and heard them, and a book of remembrance was*

> *written before him of those who feared the Lord and esteemed his name. "They shall be mine, says the Lord of hosts, in the day when I make up my treasured possession, and I will spare them as a man spares his son who serves him. Then once more you shall see the distinction between the righteous and the wicked, between one who serves God and one who does not serve him." ~ Malachi 3:16-18*

These conversations are important. Our Christian growth and fellowship with Christ find fruitful avenues when we speak the truth in love with one another.

The exploration of our Christian life is of paramount importance. We live and move in this world with one primary agenda—to glorify God in all we do. Many Christians have adopted practices and adapted their

Christian thinking to more readily conform to the world at large. But the Scripture warns against it.

> *Do not be conformed to this world, but be transformed by the renewal of your mind, that by testing you may discern what is the will of God, what is good and acceptable and perfect. ~ Romans 12:2*

You may not agree with some of the conclusions I have shared. That's okay. I didn't write this so you would agree with me but that you would strive to find your own heart open to the greatest conversation of your life, with God through His word.

So, if you have been moved to listen to God's word, if you have been inspired to ask questions and seek real answers, if the flame of exploration has been rekindled in your heart, then I implore you to do as I did—open the Bible, ask your questions and seek God's wisdom for every aspect of your life. It is there for the knowing.

Also, find yourself gathered often with the fellowship of the redeemed, the church. Make it a practice to enter into discussions on matters of Biblical importance.

And if you have made it to the very end of this book, let me say thank you. I hope and pray that you will discover in your own heart a strong desire to seek conversations on the Christian life.

In His Grace,

Michael

Connect with Michael Duncan

You can find Michael at his website:

www.authormichaelduncan.com

Or connect with him on Facebook:

www.facebook.com/michaelduncanbooks

Michael is a pastor, author, speaker and former radio co-host on the Alive in Christ radio network and has shared God's word across the country.

To invite Michael to speak at your event, simply go to:

www.authormichaelduncan.com/bookings

For a full list of his books, you can find his author's page on Amazon.com at:

www.amazon.com/michaelduncan/e/B001KML8AS

www.ingramcontent.com/pod-product-compliance
Lightning Source LLC
LaVergne TN
LVHW050544160826
845677LV00011B/2176

* 9 7 9 8 5 3 3 0 9 0 8 0 3 *